MAKING MATHS
MEANINGFUL

A Student's Workbook
for Mathematics
in Class 6

Jamie York

Floris
Books

Contents

First published in the United States of America
by Jamie York Press, Boulder, CO in 2009
www.JamieYorkPress.com
First published in the UK by Floris Books, Edinburgh in 2016
(adapted from the 2015 American edition)
Second printing 2021
© 2009 Jamie York
UK edition © 2016 Floris Books

Floris Books supports sustainable forest management
by printing this book on materials made from wood that
comes from responsible sources and reclaimed material

MIX
Paper from
responsible sources
FSC® C007785

To the Student (and Parent)

Class 6 is an important year for developing maths skills. All your work on maths this year will help to prepare you for studying maths in Class 7, Class 8, and in the upper school. How good you will become at maths depends less on natural ability and more on your effort, determination, and organisational skills. Even students who feel that they aren't good at maths can catch up by putting forth some extra effort. Don't give up! Almost anyone can become good at maths if they really want to.

Here are some tips on how to use this workbook successfully:

- Make sure your work is readable and easy to follow.
- If there isn't enough room on the worksheet, then show your work on a separate sheet of paper, making sure you write down the worksheet number and problem number, so you can easily find it later.
- If you get stuck on one problem, go on to another problem, and come back later to the one that you were stuck on.
- While working on a problem from one worksheet, it may be helpful to refer back to a problem that you did on a previous worksheet.
- *Fractions.* All answers to fraction problems should be reduced. Don't give answers as improper fractions, but convert them to mixed numbers (for example, leave your final answer as $3\frac{1}{4}$ instead of $\frac{13}{4}$).
- *Division.* Answers for division problems may be rounded to three significant digits, unless the problem states you should leave your answer as an exact decimal, in which case you must continue until it repeats or ends. For example, $2579 \div 56$ has an exact answer of $46.053\overline{571428}$. Rounding it to three significant digits means that we go only as far as the fourth digit (which is the second place after the decimal point, and is a 5 in this case), and then round up the previous digit for an answer of 46.1.
- *Answers involving time.* Answers requiring a measure of time should be given in separated units. Examples of this are: 1 day 6 hours instead of 1.25 days, and 3 hours 12 minutes instead of 3.2 hours.
- *Maths tricks.* A list of the maths tricks can be found at the back of this workbook.
- Try your best on every problem. Struggling and overcoming frustration are part of the process of doing maths. Even if you don't get a problem correct, you will learn by trying it, and then later seeing a correct solution.
- Learn from your mistakes! When you get a problem wrong, make sure you follow up on it; find your mistake, and learn how to do the problem correctly.

Getting help. The problems in this workbook are based upon the material found in our book, *A Teacher's Source Book for Teaching Mathematics in Classes 6–8.* The book has helpful explanations and examples, and is useful for parents (or tutors) who are helping their children with the worksheets found in this workbook.

Sheet 1

Do it in your head

1) 80×70

2) 400×60

3) 5000×400

4) 120×7

5) 1100×7000

6) $3600 \div 900$

7) $42,000 \div 70$

8) $720,000 \div 120,000$

9) $48,000 \div 8$

10) $54 + 8$

11) $60 - 13$

12) $73 + 24$

13) $700 - 8$

14) $687 + 36$

15) $4000 - 38$

Arithmetic
Show your work

16) $$5674 - 839$$

17) $$64,008 - 28,285$$

18) $$782 \times 539$$

19) $$587,900 \times 76,300$$

20)
$$
\begin{array}{r}
375 \\
684 \\
39 \\
865 \\
421 \\
997 \\
+\ 516 \\
\end{array}
$$

Fractions

21) $\frac{3}{11} + \frac{4}{11}$

22) $\frac{3}{8} + \frac{1}{2}$

23) $\frac{7}{12} - \frac{1}{12}$

24) $\frac{2}{3} \times \frac{3}{5}$

25) $\frac{3}{8} \times \frac{6}{7}$

26) $\frac{11}{12} \div \frac{2}{3}$

27) $\frac{5}{16} + \frac{1}{4}$

28) $\frac{7}{12} - \frac{1}{4}$

29) $\frac{45}{49} \times \frac{21}{25}$

30) $\frac{3}{16} + \frac{7}{12}$

Reduce each fraction

31) $\frac{6}{9}$

32) $\frac{30}{120}$

33) $\frac{35}{49}$

34) $\frac{24}{60}$

35) $\frac{36}{270}$

36) $\frac{175}{225}$

37) $\frac{540}{2880}$

Division

Hints:

- The second number goes outside 'the house'.
- All division problems on this sheet work out exactly.

38) $3456 \div 6$

39) $48{,}424 \div 8$

40) $5394 \div 62$

41) $49{,}441 \div 49$

Sheet 2

Do it in your head

1) 60×90

2) 500×120

3) $36{,}000 \div 600$

4) $42{,}000 \div 70$

5) $60{,}000 \div 2{,}000$

6) $34 + 28$

7) $70 - 33$

8) $83 + 56$

9) $700 - 36$

10) 7.2×1000

11) $7.2 \div 1000$

12) 0.054×100

Arithmetic

Show your work.

13)
$$
\begin{array}{r}
732 \\
674 \\
789 \\
468 \\
927 \\
+\ 316 \\
\end{array}
$$

14)
$$
\begin{array}{r}
50{,}607 \\
-\ 18{,}639 \\
\end{array}
$$

15)
$$
\begin{array}{r}
32 \\
\times 11 \\
\end{array}
$$

16)
$$
\begin{array}{r}
35 \\
\times 11 \\
\end{array}
$$

17)
$$
\begin{array}{r}
43 \\
\times 11 \\
\end{array}
$$

18) By looking at Nos. 15, 16 and 17, what is the trick for multiplying by 11?

Cast out nines to check your answer. Ignore ending zeros

19)
$$
\begin{array}{r}
765{,}300 \\
\times\ \ 82{,}600 \\
\end{array}
$$

20)
$$
\begin{array}{r}
4785 \\
\times 1589 \\
\end{array}
$$

Reduce each fraction

21) $\frac{2}{8}$

22) $\frac{14}{35}$

23) $\frac{3600}{4500}$

24) $\frac{48}{600}$

Decimals

25) $87.5 + 7.35$

26) $302.47 - 4.6$

27) $51.8 - 4.26$

28) $212 - 0.03$

Fractions

29) $\frac{2}{15} + \frac{4}{15}$

30) $\frac{4}{5} + \frac{2}{15}$

31) $\frac{7}{11} - \frac{3}{5}$

32) $\frac{5}{12} - \frac{3}{20}$

33) $\frac{3}{8} \div \frac{6}{7}$

34) $\frac{3}{4} \times \frac{14}{15}$

35) $\frac{15}{16} \times \frac{20}{21}$

36) $\frac{8}{12} \div \frac{49}{77}$

Division

Leave your answers as mixed numbers (e.g. $3\frac{2}{5}$), and use short division if the divisor is only one digit. Show your work on a separate sheet, if needed.

37) $3745 \div 4$

38) $25{,}257 \div 9$

39) $4300 \div 63$

40) $32{,}900 \div 81$

Make flashcards

Your teacher should tell you which of the multiplication facts below you need to make into flashcards. You should practice them every day until two weeks past the point that you know them really well, and then continue practicing them once per week. This will help you to do calculations quickly and accurately in the years ahead.

2 × 2 = 4	8 × 2 = 16	12 × 2 = 24
3 × 2 = 6	8 × 3 = 24	12 × 3 = 36
3 × 3 = 9	8 × 4 = 32	12 × 4 = 48
4 × 2 = 8	8 × 5 = 40	12 × 5 = 60
4 × 3 = 12	8 × 6 = 48	12 × 6 = 72
4 × 4 = 16	8 × 7 = 56	12 × 7 = 84
	8 × 8 = 64	12 × 8 = 96
5 × 2 = 10		12 × 9 = 108
5 × 3 = 15	9 × 2 = 18	12 × 11 = 132
5 × 4 = 20	9 × 3 = 27	12 × 12 = 144
5 × 5 = 25	9 × 4 = 36	
	9 × 5 = 45	13 × 2 = 26
6 × 2 = 12	9 × 6 = 54	13 × 3 = 39
6 × 3 = 18	9 × 7 = 63	13 × 4 = 52
6 × 4 = 24	9 × 8 = 72	13 × 13 = 169
6 × 5 = 30	9 × 9 = 81	
6 × 6 = 36		14 × 2 = 28
	11 × 2 = 22	14 × 3 = 42
7 × 2 = 14	11 × 3 = 33	14 × 14 = 196
7 × 3 = 21	11 × 4 = 44	
7 × 4 = 28	11 × 5 = 55	15 × 2 = 30
7 × 5 = 35	11 × 6 = 66	15 × 3 = 45
7 × 6 = 42	11 × 7 = 77	15 × 4 = 60
7 × 7 = 49	11 × 8 = 88	15 × 5 = 75
	11 × 9 = 99	15 × 15 = 225
	11 × 11 = 121	

16 × 2 = 32	
16 × 3 = 48	
16 × 4 = 64	
16 × 16 = 256	
18 × 2 = 36	
18 × 18 = 324	
25 × 2 = 50	
25 × 3 = 75	
25 × 4 = 100	
25 × 5 = 125	
25 × 6 = 150	
25 × 25 = 625	

Optional:

13 × 5 = 65	
14 × 4 = 56	
14 × 5 = 70	
16 × 5 = 80	
18 × 3 = 54	
18 × 4 = 72	
18 × 5 = 90	
25 × 8 = 200	

Sheet 3

Do it in your head

1) 60 × 400

2) 500 × 800

3) 45,000 ÷ 5000

4) 720,000 ÷ 800

5) 84 + 38

6) 2000 − 38

7) 2851.2 ÷ 1000

8) 0.45 ÷ 1000

9) 0.0003 × 100

10) 11 × 42

11) 11 × 76

12) 110 × 930

13) 16 × 4

14) 150×4

15) 749
     524
     602
     347
     996
     283
    +418

Decimals

16) $30.5 + 5.26$

17) $92.4 - 0.286$

18) $51.893 - 4.26$

19) 0.04×0.7

20) 0.006×0.03

21) 6×0.03

22) 0.06×8000

23) 0.07×2.3

Cast out nines to check your answer

24)   7,823,000
     $\times$ 95,600

25)   4.38
     $\times$ 0.974

Reduce each fraction

26) $\frac{540}{720}$

27) $\frac{280}{44,000}$

Fractions

28) $\frac{7}{10} + \frac{2}{25}$

29) $\frac{27}{37} + \frac{9}{37}$

30) $\frac{3}{8} \div \frac{11}{16}$

31) $\frac{18}{25} \times \frac{15}{16}$

32) Convert to a mixed number (e.g. $3\frac{2}{5}$).

   a) $\frac{23}{3}$

   b) $\frac{77}{12}$

33) Convert to an improper fraction (e.g. $\frac{12}{7}$)

   a) $5\frac{2}{3}$

   b) $11\frac{7}{8}$

Long division

Example: $280{,}139 \div 583$

With difficult divisors like 583 we should not first ask ourselves, 'How many times does 583 go into 2801?' but rather, we round 583 to 600, drop off the zeros, and then ask the easier question, 'How many times does 6 go into 28?' The answer to this question is 4, so we estimate that 4 is the first digit in our answer (it may be off by one) and then we multiply 4 times 583 to see if it works.

```
         4
583 ) 280139
     -2332
      ─────
       469
```

Since 469 is less than 583, we can tell that 4 is correct as the first digit of our answer. After bringing down the 3, we then find the next digit in our answer by asking, 'How many times does 6 go into 47?' (Notice that we rounded 46 to 47 because the next digit, 9, was 5 or greater.) The answer to this question is 7, so we estimate that 7 is the next digit in our answer.

```
        47
583 ) 280139
     -2332
      ─────
       4693
      -4081
       ─────
        612
```

But since 612 is greater than 583, we know that 7 is too small. So instead, we try 8 as the second digit, which works fine.

```
        48
583 ) 280139
     -2332
      ─────
       4693
      -4664
       ─────
         29
```

(This problem is unfinished.)

Fill in the blanks

34) With $3745 \div 738$, we first ask, 'How many times does _____ go into ____?'

35) With $45{,}800 \div 76$, we first ask, 'How many times does _____ go into ____?'

36) With $92{,}538 \div 274$, we first ask, 'How many times does _____ go into ____?'

Now, using your above answers, do the division problems below. Leave your answers as mixed numbers. Show your work on a separate piece of paper.

37) $3745 \div 738$

38) $45{,}800 \div 76$

39) $92{,}538 \div 274$

Short division

40) $6583 \div 4$

41) $26{,}618 \div 7$

Mixed numbers

42) $4\frac{7}{11} + 3\frac{8}{11}$

43) $8\frac{5}{12} + 9\frac{7}{8}$

Sheet 4

Do it in your head

1) 500×6000

2) 40×9000

3) $56{,}000 \div 70$

4) $55{,}000 \div 1{,}100$

5) 0.007×100

6) $0.007 \div 100$

7) 51.2×1000

8) $72.3 \div 1000$

9) 11×45

10) 11×85

11) 45×4

12) 520×4

13)
```
  587
  677
  797
  147
  537
  467
  927
+ 317
```

14) 0.03×0.7

15) 0.005×0.04

Decimals

16) $586.3 + 5.72$

17) $70.4 - 6.82$

18) 103×107

19) 104×107

20) 105×109

21) Look at the previous three problems. What is the trick for multiplying two numbers that are just over 100?

22) Cast out nines to check your answer.

$$789.2$$
$$\times\ 5.34$$

23) 8^2

24) 2^3

25) 40^2

26) 10^5

Fractions

27) $\frac{4}{5} + \frac{2}{7}$

28) $\frac{4}{5} - \frac{1}{5}$

29) $\frac{8}{9} \div \frac{6}{7}$

30) $\frac{5}{12} \times \frac{8}{15}$

31) $5\frac{7}{8} + 12\frac{2}{3}$

32) $7\frac{7}{8} - 2\frac{5}{8}$

33) $7\frac{5}{8} - 2\frac{7}{8}$

34) $7\frac{3}{8} - 2\frac{4}{5}$

35) Convert to a mixed number:
$$\frac{75}{8}$$

36) Convert to an improper fraction:
$$7\frac{3}{8}$$

Short division
Leave your answer as a mixed number.

37) $867 \div 5$

38) $62{,}794 \div 7$

Long division

Fill in the blanks. If necessary, review the example and problems on the previous worksheet.

39) With $3497 \div 81$, we first ask, 'How many times does _____ go into ____?'

40) With $18{,}457 \div 683$, we first ask, 'How many times does _____ go into ____?'

41) With $91.35 \div 72.5$, we first ask, 'How many times does _____ go into ____?'

Now, using your answers above, do the division problems below. Leave your answers as mixed numbers. Show your work on a separate piece of paper.

42) $3497 \div 81$

43) $18{,}457 \div 683$

44) Leave your answer as a decimal: $91.35 \div 72.5$

Sheet 5

Do it in your head

1) 800×900

2) $40{,}000 \div 80$

3) 74.5×1000

4) $7.31 \div 100$

5) 11×23

6) 110×96

7) 17×4

8) 550×4

9) 7×0.005

10) 0.012×0.04

11) $6800 \div 4$

12) $140 \div 4$

13) 106×104

14) 107×108

15) 104×105

16) 9^2

17) 700^2

18) $\frac{3}{5} + \frac{2}{5}$

19) $\frac{5}{8} \times \frac{8}{15}$

20) $\frac{3}{7} \times \frac{2}{7}$

21) $\frac{4}{15} \div \frac{2}{5}$

22) $4 - 0.3$

Multiplication facts
(Have you been practising your flashcards?)

23) 13×3

24) 14×2

25) 25×3

26) 13×13

27) 15×5

28) 25×5

29) 16×2

30) 13×2

31) 16×3

32) 25×6

33) 15×3

34) 14×14

35) 25×4

36) 16×4

37) 15×15

38) 25×2

39) 16×16

40) 14×3

41) 13×4

42) 15×2

43) 18×18

44) 15×4

45) 18×2

46) 25×25

Decimals

47) $56.32 + 0.004$

48) Cast out nines to check your answer.

$$\begin{array}{r} 3{,}896{,}000 \\ \times \quad 57{,}400 \\ \hline \end{array}$$

49) $56.32 - 0.004$

50) $(0.032)^2$

Short division
51) Leave your answer as a mixed number:
$4739 \div 8$

52) Leave your answer as a decimal:
$180{,}247 \div 3$

Long division
Fix the divisor. Make the divisor easier by getting rid of the decimal or the ending zeros. Do not actually divide yet.
   Example: $735.48 \div 8.3$
   Here we change the problem to $7354.8 \div 83$.
   Example: $528.3 \div 2600$
   Here we change the problem to $5.283 \div 26$.

53) $21.3 \div 5.68$
   We change it to:

54) $687.4 \div 37{,}000$
   We change it to:

55) $7 \div 0.097$
   We change it to:

For the next three problems, show your work on a separate sheet.
Now, consider the answers that you just gave and do each division problem. Give your answers as decimals, and stop at four significant digits.

56) $21.3 \div 5.68$

57) $687.4 \div 37{,}000$

58) $7 \div 0.097$

Fractions

59) $\dfrac{41}{5} + \dfrac{10}{15}$

60) $\dfrac{7}{20} + \dfrac{11}{15}$

61) $\dfrac{5}{8} \times \dfrac{6}{7}$

62) $\dfrac{5}{6} \div \dfrac{5}{12}$

63) $9\dfrac{5}{7} + 4\dfrac{3}{4}$

64) $16\dfrac{2}{5} - 6\dfrac{3}{4}$

65) $7\dfrac{2}{5} - 2\dfrac{2}{15}$

66) $4\dfrac{1}{2} \times 1\dfrac{1}{3}$

67) $6\dfrac{2}{3} \times 2\dfrac{3}{4}$

68) Two hours is how many seconds?

69) What is 2^{20}?

70) *Challenge*
   Continuing from 2^{20}, calculate powers of 2, as high as you can go, perhaps as high as 2^{100}. It is advisable to check with your teacher after each exponent of 10 (e.g. 2^{20}, 2^{30}, etc.) to make sure your answer is correct before moving on.

Sheet 6

Do it in your head

1) 1200×600

2) $48{,}000 \div 8{,}000$

3) 4.532×100

4) $932.3 \div 100$

5) 11×89

6) 110×46

7) 350×4

8) 215×4

9) 0.06×0.05

10) 0.002×0.04

11) $1800 \div 4$

12) $82 \div 4$

13) 106×112

14) 102×103

15) 1.15×1.02

16) 2^3

17) 3000^2

18) $\frac{1}{3} + \frac{1}{5}$

19) $\frac{5}{6} \times \frac{9}{10}$

20) $\frac{7}{12} \times \frac{5}{12}$

21) $\frac{7}{12} + \frac{5}{12}$

22) $11.5 - 0.24$

Multiplication facts
(Have you memorised these?)

23) 16×3

24) 13^2

25) 14×3

26) 15×5

27) 13×3

28) 18^2

29) 14^2

30) 25×3

31) 18×2

32) 13×4

33) 25×5

34) 16^2

35) 15^2

36) 25^2

Fractions & decimals

37) $512.7 + 6.48$

Making Maths Meaningful

38) $80.4 - 3.47$

39) $(0.0087)^2$

40) $(0.02)^5$

41) $(3\frac{2}{3})^2$

42) Convert to mixed numbers: $\frac{65}{9}$

43) Convert to an improper fraction: $8\frac{4}{9}$

44) $\frac{5}{6} + \frac{5}{8}$

45) $\frac{48}{49} \times \frac{35}{36}$

46) $5\frac{1}{2} \times 3\frac{2}{3}$

47) $5\frac{1}{2} \div 3\frac{2}{3}$

48) $3\frac{2}{3} \div 5\frac{1}{2}$

49) $3\frac{3}{4} \times \frac{17}{3}$

Short division
50) Leave your answer as a mixed number.
$35,451 \div 6$

Long division
Fix the divisor. Make the divisor easier by getting rid of the decimal or the ending zeros. Do not actually divide yet. (See examples on the previous worksheet, if necessary.)

51) $700 \div 6.6$
We change it to:

52) $41.7736 \div 0.047$
We change it to:

53) $8.39 \div 1800$
We change it to:

Divide. Leave your answers as exact decimals (perhaps repeating).

54) $700 \div 6.6$

55) $41.7736 \div 0.047$

56) $8.39 \div 1800$

57)
$$\begin{array}{r} 784 \\ 269 \\ 928 \\ 76 \\ 841 \\ 797 \\ + 473 \\ \hline \end{array}$$

58) Betty earns £235 per week (after tax). After 5 weeks of work, she put £641 of her earnings into her savings account and then evenly divided the rest between her three sisters. How much did each sister get?

Convert to decimals

59) Convert each fraction into an equal decimal. Divide when necessary.

$\frac{1}{2} =$ $\frac{1}{8} =$

$\frac{1}{3} =$ $\frac{3}{8} =$

$\frac{2}{3} =$ $\frac{5}{8} =$

$\frac{1}{4} =$ $\frac{7}{8} =$

$\frac{3}{4} =$ $\frac{1}{9} =$

$\frac{1}{5} =$ $\frac{2}{9} =$

$\frac{2}{5} =$ $\frac{4}{9} =$

$\frac{3}{5} =$ $\frac{5}{9} =$

$\frac{4}{5} =$ $\frac{7}{9} =$

$\frac{1}{6} =$ $\frac{8}{9} =$

$\frac{5}{6} =$

Sheet 7

Do it in your head

1) 30×7000

2) $36,000 \div 40$

3) $8.03 \times 10,000$

4) $8.03 \div 100$

5) 11×62

6) 320×4

7) 0.3×0.007

8) $140 \div 4$

9) 105×103

10) 10.9×1.11

11) 90^2

12) $(0.01)^3$

13) $\frac{2}{9} + \frac{4}{9}$

14) $\frac{3}{20} \times \frac{5}{6}$

15) $\frac{2}{9} + \frac{1}{3}$

16) $\frac{3}{4} \div \frac{3}{8}$

17) $\dfrac{\frac{3}{4}}{\frac{3}{8}}$

18) $17 - 2.3$

19) $304 - 298$

20) $703 - 697$

21) $4005 - 3996$

Fractions

22) $\frac{3}{4} - \frac{11}{18}$

23) $\frac{42}{49} \times \frac{33}{44}$

24) $(2\frac{1}{2})^2$

25) $(10\frac{2}{5})^2$

26) $2\frac{2}{5} + 1\frac{7}{8}$

27) $2\frac{2}{5} - 1\frac{7}{8}$

28) $2\frac{2}{5} \times 1\frac{7}{8}$

29) $2\frac{2}{5} \div 1\frac{7}{8}$

30) $2\frac{2}{3} \times 6\frac{3}{4}$

Short division

31) Fix the divisor and then leave the answer as an exact decimal (perhaps repeating).

$748.4 \div 0.09$

32) Cast out nines to check your answer.

$$\begin{array}{r} 67.39 \\ \times\, 0.00874 \\ \hline \end{array}$$

Estimate

Without doing any exact calculation, circle the closest answer. Try to come up with your answer as fast as possible.

33) $6953 + 5197$
  a) 10,000
  b) 11,000
  c) 12,000
  d) 13,000

34) $805,946 - 597,265$
  a) 200,000
  b) 300,000
  c) 400,000
  d) 500,000

35) 802×489
  a) 30,000
  b) 40,000
  c) 50,000
  d) 300,000
  e) 400,000
  f) 500,000

36) $58,374 \div 29$
  a) 200
  b) 300
  c) 2000
  d) 3000
  e) 20,000

Long division

Fix the divisor and then divide. Leave your answers as exact decimals (perhaps repeating).

37) $7 \div 22000$

38) $6.52 \div 0.0074$

39) Leave the answer as a mixed number:
  $3285 \div 37$

40) Beth bought 3½ kg of bananas for 84p per kg, a carton of ice cream for £2.35, and had to pay 5p for a plastic bag. How much change did she get if she gave the cashier a £10 note?

Square roots
Example: $\sqrt{4900} = 70$

41) $\sqrt{16}$

42) $\sqrt{144}$

43) $\sqrt{900}$

44) $\sqrt{3600}$

45) $\sqrt{10,000}$

46) $\sqrt{4,000,000}$

47) *New flashcards*
Review all the decimal-to-fraction conversions given in the last problem of the previous worksheet. Make a new flashcard for each of these conversion facts.

Sheet 8

Do it in your head

1) 500×1200

2) $30,000 \div 500$

3) 0.053×100

4) $973.1 \div 10$

5) 11×560

6) 0.45×4

7) 1.2×1.1

8) $300 \div 4$

9) 107×112

10) 1200^2

11) 10^4

12) $(0.05)^2$

13) $\frac{7}{8} + \frac{1}{4}$

14) $\frac{7}{10} \times \frac{5}{6}$

15) $\frac{2}{5} \div \frac{3}{5}$

16) $\dfrac{\frac{2}{5}}{\frac{3}{5}}$

17) $\left(\frac{3}{5}\right)^2$

18) $\sqrt{81}$

19) $\sqrt{64}$

20) $\sqrt{2500}$

21) $\sqrt{\dfrac{16}{49}}$

22) $34 - 1.9$

23) $813 - 795$

24) $6025 - 5998$

25) 13^2

26) 16×4

27) 25×6

28) 13×4

29) 15^2

30) 15×5

31) 14^2

32) Convert to a decimal:
  a) $\dfrac{2}{5}$

  b) $\dfrac{3}{4}$

  c) $\dfrac{1}{3}$

  d) $\dfrac{5}{8}$

  e) $\dfrac{1}{6}$

  f) $\dfrac{4}{9}$

  g) $\dfrac{3}{5}$

33) Convert to a fraction:
  a) 0.5

  b) 0.8

  c) 0.125

  d) $0.\overline{5}$

  e) $0.\overline{6}$

Fractions

34) $\dfrac{5}{6} - \dfrac{3}{8}$

35) $\left(3\dfrac{3}{5}\right)^2$

36) $312\dfrac{2}{5} - 309\dfrac{2}{3}$

37) $4\dfrac{1}{6} \div \dfrac{5}{9}$

38)
```
    485
    738
    628
    395
   6897
    274
 +  739
```

Estimate

Without doing any exact calculation, circle the closest answer, and state whether the exact answer is *greater than* or *less than* the circled answer.

39) 39,064 + 28,925
   a) 50,000
   b) 60,000
   c) 70,000
   d) 80,000

40) 7178 − 3943
   a) 2,000
   b) 3,000
   c) 4,000
   d) 5,000

41) 8197 × 7026
   a) 56,000
   b) 63,000
   c) 560,000
   d) 630,000
   e) 56,000,000
   f) 63,000,000

42) 24,257 ÷ 39
   a) 60
   b) 80
   c) 600
   d) 800
   e) 6000
   f) 8000

Divisibility

State whether each of the following numbers is evenly divisible by 2, 3, 4, 5, 9, or 10.

43) 3622

44) 687,528

45) 58,395

46) 90,472,550

Discover the trick

Convert each fraction into a decimal. Divide only if you need to. Try to discover the trick for yourself, so that you don't have to divide for all of them.

47) Twentieths

   a) $\frac{7}{20}$

   b) $\frac{3}{20}$

   c) $\frac{9}{20}$

   d) $\frac{11}{20}$

48) Elevenths

   a) $\frac{7}{11}$

   b) $\frac{3}{11}$

   c) $\frac{9}{11}$

   d) $\frac{6}{11}$

49) Ninths, etc.

   a) $\frac{7}{9}$

   b) $\frac{4}{9}$

   c) $\frac{14}{99}$

   d) $\frac{58}{99}$

   e) $\frac{374}{999}$

   f) $\frac{176}{999}$

   g) $\frac{7}{99}$

Short division

50) Leave your answer as an exact decimal.
    $3079 \div 40$

51) Jill bought 12 apples at 26p each and 4.2 kg of bananas at 85p per kg, and had to pay 5p for a plastic bag. She gave the cashier a £10 note, a 20p coin and 4 pennies. How much change did she get?

Why did she give the 20p and four 1p coins?

Long division

52) Leave your answer rounded to three significant digits.
    $0.3 \div 37.1$

53) Convert the following improper fraction to both a mixed number and an exact decimal.
    $$\frac{6231}{88}$$

Sheet 9

Do it in your head

1) $\sqrt{400}$

2) $70 \div 4$

3) 25×2

4) $2005 - 1987$

5) $0.006 \div 0.002$

6) 15×3

7) 25×4

8) 200^3

9) $(0.004)^2$

10) $\frac{5}{7} \times \frac{3}{11}$

11) 400×80

12) $\frac{3}{5} \div \frac{2}{3}$

13) $\frac{\frac{3}{5}}{\frac{2}{3}}$

14) $0.03 \div 100$

15) $\sqrt{1{,}440{,}000}$

16) 25×5

17) 15×2

18) 0.03×1000

19) 25×3

20) $\sqrt{\frac{9}{400}}$

21) 15×4

22) $3.2 \div 0.08$

23) 980×11

24) $\frac{3}{10} + \frac{1}{5}$

25) 13×3

26) 25^2

Convert to decimals

Some of these you should have memorised, for others (20ths, 11ths, 9ths, 99ths, etc.) there are tricks, and for the rest you'll have to divide.

27) a) ¼

b) $\frac{7}{8}$

c) $\frac{7}{9}$

d) $\frac{3}{20}$

e) $\frac{3}{4}$

f) $\frac{1}{5}$

g) $\frac{3}{8}$

h) $\frac{83}{99}$

i) $\frac{8}{11}$

j) $\frac{11}{40}$

k) $\frac{4}{5}$

l) $\frac{19}{20}$

m) $\frac{6}{11}$

n) $\frac{19}{30}$

28) Cast out nines to check your answer.

$$\begin{array}{r} 857{,}900 \\ \times\ 584{,}000 \\ \hline \end{array}$$

Estimate

Round the numbers in the problem to one or two significant digits, then estimate the answer.

29) $8273 + 6187$

30) 719×382

31) $39{,}657 - 28{,}053$

32) $81{,}956 \div 39$

Divisibility

State whether each of the following numbers is evenly divisible by 2, 3, 4, 5, 9, or 10.

33) $85{,}734$

34) $85{,}741{,}920$

Fractions

35) $\frac{16}{25} + \frac{14}{15}$

36) $7\frac{4}{5} \div 3\frac{1}{4}$

37) $\dfrac{7\frac{4}{5}}{3\frac{1}{4}}$

38) $657\frac{8}{9} - 652\frac{2}{3}$

39) $(3\frac{1}{3})^3$

Unit cost

40) Nine red pens cost £5.13, and eleven green pens cost £6.49. Which one has a cheaper unit price?

41) Five kg of oranges cost £12.05. What is the cost of seven kg of oranges?

Short division

42) Leave your answer as an exact decimal: 76,941 ÷ 800

Long division

43) Leave your answer rounded to three significant digits.
57.2 ÷ 4.83

44) Convert the following improper fraction to both a mixed number and an exact decimal.
$\dfrac{7671}{37}$

Powers

45) $2^3 =$ $3^3 =$

$2^4 =$ $3^4 =$

$2^5 =$ $3^5 =$

$2^6 =$ $3^6 =$

$2^7 =$ $5^3 =$

$2^8 =$ $5^4 =$

$2^9 =$

$2^{10} =$ $6^3 =$

$4^3 =$ $7^3 =$

$4^4 =$ $8^3 =$

$4^5 =$ $9^3 =$

Sheet 10

Do it in your head

1) 18×2

2) $914 - 888$

3) 16×3

4) $(1.2)^2$

5) $\frac{5}{18} \div \frac{5}{9}$

6) $\frac{\frac{5}{18}}{\frac{5}{9}}$

7) $\sqrt{90,000}$

8) 16×4

9) 18^2

10) $\frac{11}{12} \times \frac{36}{11}$

11) 3.15×4

12) 14×2

13) $\sqrt{1.21}$

14) 16×2

15) $72,000 \div 60$

16) 109×105

17) $\frac{9}{10} - \frac{1}{3}$

18) 14×3

19) 16^2

Convert to decimals

Each problem either has a trick or should be memorised.

20) a) $\frac{2}{9}$

   b) $\frac{1}{20}$

   c) $\frac{9}{20}$

   d) $\frac{2}{3}$

   e) $\frac{3}{5}$

   f) $\frac{7}{10}$

   g) $\frac{59}{100}$

   h) $\frac{1}{8}$

   i) $\frac{5}{11}$

   j) $\frac{5}{9}$

   k) $\frac{68}{99}$

   l) $\frac{713}{999}$

   m) $\frac{9}{11}$

   n) $\frac{5}{6}$

   o) $\frac{5}{8}$

   p) $\frac{13}{20}$

21) Discover the trick.

   a) 7×99

   b) 4×999

c) 5×9999

d) $3 \times 99{,}999$

Estimate
Round the numbers in the problem to one or two significant digits, then estimate the answer.

22) $685{,}036 + 725{,}672$

23) 2276×807

24) $81{,}763 - 69{,}627$

25) $48{,}753 \div 716$

Unit cost
26) Five light bulbs cost £3.40. How much do eight light bulbs cost?

27) Five light bulbs cost £2.45. How much do 20 light bulbs cost?

Fractions
28) $73\frac{3}{11} - 68\frac{1}{2}$

29) $\frac{5}{9} + \frac{7}{36}$

30) $\dfrac{5\frac{5}{8}}{6}$

31) $3 \div 4\frac{3}{8}$

32) $4\frac{3}{8} \times 5$

Divisibility
State whether each of the following numbers is evenly divisible by 2, 3, 4, 5, 9, or 10.

33) $81{,}945$

34) $9{,}472{,}152$

Measurement
35) 5 metres is how many centimetres?

36) 16 kilograms is how many grams?

37) 96 millilitres is how many litres?

38) 11 hours is how many minutes?

39) 3½ cm is how many mm?

40) 1.7 km is how many metres?

41) Convert the following improper fraction to both a mixed number and an exact decimal.
$$\frac{697}{24}$$

Short division

42) Leave your answer as a mixed number.
94,034 ÷ 6

New flashcards

43) Look at all the powers problems given at the end of the previous work-sheet. Make a new flashcard for each one.

Sheet 11

Do it in your head

1) 28×11

2) 13^2

3) $(50)^3$

4) 1^{12}

5) $\sqrt{3600}$

6) 13×3

7) $\dfrac{\frac{3}{4}}{\frac{5}{6}}$

8) $860 \div 4$

9) 25×4

10) $\sqrt{0.000\,025}$

11) $65.7 \div 1000$

12) 5.837×100

13) 25^2

14) $45 \div 0.05$

15) 15×5

16) Cast out nines to check your answer.
$$\begin{array}{r} 7.92 \\ \times\ 57.8 \\ \hline \end{array}$$

Decimal/fraction conversion

17) Convert to decimals. Each problem either has a trick or should be memorised.

a) $\frac{2}{5}$

b) $\frac{3}{4}$

c) $\frac{9}{10}$

d) $\frac{1}{3}$

e) $\frac{7}{99}$

f) $\frac{4}{9}$

g) $\frac{4}{11}$

h) $\frac{7}{20}$

i) $\frac{1}{6}$

j) $\frac{7}{9}$

17) k) $\frac{1}{10}$

l) $\frac{1}{11}$

m) $\frac{1}{9}$

n) $\frac{8}{9}$

o) $\frac{91}{100}$

p) $\frac{75}{999}$

q) $\frac{4}{999}$

r) $\frac{17}{20}$

18) Convert to fractions:
a) 0.5

b) 0.6

c) 0.7

d) 0.17

e) 0.75

f) $0.\overline{3}$

g) 0.125

h) $0.8\overline{3}$

i) $0.\overline{7}$

j) $0.\overline{23}$

Divisibility
State whether each of the following numbers is evenly divisible by 2, 3, 4, 5, 9, or 10.

19) 8,041,736

20) 7,485,030

Discover the trick
Convert each fraction to a decimal. Divide only if necessary. Try to discover the trick for yourself.

21) $\frac{83}{99}$

22) $\frac{83}{990}$

23) $\frac{83}{9900}$

24) $\frac{83}{990,000}$

25) $\frac{743}{999}$

26) $\frac{743}{9990}$

27) $\frac{743}{9,990,000}$

28) $\frac{4}{999}$

29) $\frac{4}{9990}$

30) $\frac{7}{900}$

31) $\frac{82}{9,999,000}$

Fractions

32) $39\frac{2}{7} + 33\frac{3}{4}$

33) $\left(2\frac{1}{2}\right)^4$

34) What is $\frac{1}{3}$ of 360?

35) What is $\frac{3}{5}$ of 45?

36) What is $\frac{5}{9}$ of 45?

37) What is $\frac{2}{3}$ of 45?

38) What is $\frac{3}{7}$ of 45?

Decimals

39) $379.4 - 6.932$

40) $(0.0079)^2$

41) $(1.1)^4$

Long division

42) What is the mistake in the problem shown below?

```
        161
  47 ) 7990
      -47
       329
      -282
        47
       -47
         0
```

Round your answers to three significant digits.

43) $2.52 \div 8200$

44) $1300 \div 6.78$

Measurement

45) 64 inches is how many feet?

46) 1116 grams is how many kilograms?

47) 4½ litres is how many millilitres?

48) 3¼ kilograms is how many grams?

49) How many yards are in one mile?

50) There are two marks made on a board, one at $17^{13}/_{16}$ inches from the end of the board, and the other at $23^{5}/_{16}$ inches from the same end. How far apart are the marks?

51) A string, 15.6 metres long, is cut into 24 equal lengths. How long (in cm) is each piece?

52) One drill bit has a diameter of $^3/_8$ in and another is $^{11}/_{32}$ in. Which one is bigger, and by how much is it bigger?

Sheet 12

Memorised facts

(Note: Convert means fractions into decimals and decimals into fractions.)

1) 14×3

2) 16^2

3) 18×2

4) 14^2

5) 16×4

6) 18^2

7) Convert $\frac{3}{5}$

8) Convert $\frac{3}{4}$

9) Convert $\frac{7}{9}$

10) Convert $\frac{5}{8}$

11) Convert $\frac{2}{3}$

12) Convert $\frac{1}{6}$

13) Convert $0.\overline{4}$

14) Convert $0.\overline{3}$

15) Convert 0.375

16) Convert $0.8\overline{3}$

17) Convert 0.8

18) 2^4

19) 3^4

20) 2^3

21) 4^3

22) 5^3

23) 2^6

24) 2^{10}

25) 4^5

26) 5^4

27) 2^5

28) 4^4

Optional:

29) 13×5

30) 18×4

31) 16×5

32) 14×4

33) 18×5

34) 25×8

35) 18×3

36) 14×5

37) 2^7

38) 3^6

39) 7^3

40) 2^9

41) 8^3

42) 2^8

43) 6^3

44) 3^5

45) 9^3

Do it in your head

46) $36,000 \div 90$

47) 4.35×4

48) 999×4

49) 9999×8

50) 102×105

51) $3045 - 2989$

52) $(0.06)^2$

53) 10^6

54) Convert $\frac{9}{10}$

55) Convert $\frac{47}{99}$

56) Convert $\frac{743}{1000}$

57) Convert $\frac{29}{1000}$

58) Convert $\frac{29}{999}$

59) Convert $\frac{873}{99,900}$

60) Convert $\frac{7}{99,900}$

61) Convert $\frac{7}{10,000}$

62) Convert $\frac{7}{9000}$

63) Convert $\frac{59}{9990}$

Estimate

64) 5826×394

65) $673,989 \div 718$

66) $85,045 + 28,495$

Fractions

67) $\frac{39}{8} + 13\frac{5}{8}$

68) $\frac{4\frac{1}{2}}{\frac{4}{5}}$

69) What is $\frac{1}{6}$ of 24?

70) What is $\frac{2}{5}$ of 5500?

71) What is $\frac{2}{3}$ of 4?

72) What is $\frac{3}{8}$ of 280?

73) What is half of $\frac{4}{7}$?

74) What is half of $\frac{5}{11}$?

75) What is $\frac{4}{9}$ doubled?

76) What is $\frac{3}{8}$ doubled?

Formulas

Temperature conversion formulas:

$$C = \frac{5}{9} \times (F - 32)$$
$$F = \frac{9}{5} \times C + 32$$

77) What is 59°F in Celsius?

78) What is 30°C in Fahrenheit?

79) What is 212°F in Celsius?

Division

80) Leave your answer as a mixed number.
    $62,223 \div 8$

81) Leave your answer as an exact decimal.
    $87.5 \div 4.44$

Measurement

82) 240 cm is how many metres?

83) 2½ litres is how many millilitres?

84) 2 tons is how many grams?

85) A string is cut into two pieces measuring 2¾ metres and 3½ metres. How long was the original string?

86) One board is 14⅝ inches long, and another board is 22¼ inches long. How much longer is the second board?

Unit cost

87) 5 kg of bananas cost £4.30. How much do 15 kg of bananas cost?

88) Which is a better deal: spring water sold at 89p for a 1.5 litre bottle, or spring water sold at £2.30 for a pack of twelve 330 millilitre bottles?

Sheet 13

Memorised facts

1) 13×4

2) 25×6

3) 15^2

4) Convert $\frac{2}{5}$

5) Convert $\frac{5}{6}$

6) Convert $\frac{1}{8}$

7) Convert $0.\overline{6}$

8) Convert $0.\overline{1}$

9) Convert 0.75

10) 2^3 *2·2·2*   *8*

11) 3^3 *3·3·3*   *27*

12) 4^3

13) 5^3

14) 2^{10}

15) 5^4 *5·5·5·5*

16) 2^5

17) 4^5

Optional:

18) 18×4

19) 16×5

20) 14×4

21) 8^3

22) 2^8

23) 3^5

Do it in your head

24) 800×50

25) $356.2 \div 100$

26) 1.1×5.8

27) $3000 \div 4$

28) $(0.12)^2$

29) $\sqrt{\dfrac{16}{25}}$

30) $0.15 \div 0.003$

31) 7×99

32) $6 \times 99{,}999$

33) $600 \div 800$

34) $28 \div 35$

35) $18{,}000 \div 81{,}000$

36) Convert $\frac{41}{100}$

37) Convert $\frac{208}{999}$

38) Convert $\frac{11}{20}$

39) Convert $\frac{10}{11}$

40) Convert $\frac{43}{999}$

41) Convert $\frac{43}{9990}$

42) Convert $\frac{7}{99,000}$

43) Convert 0.83

44) Convert 0.083

45) Convert $0.\overline{83}$

46) Convert $0.\overline{083}$

47) Convert $0.0\overline{83}$

48) Convert $0.00\overline{083}$

Divisibility

State whether each of the following numbers is evenly divisible by 2, 3, 4, 5, 9, or 10.

49) 609,348

50) 86,175

Division

51) Leave your answer as an exact decimal.
$87.1 \div 16,000$

Fractions

52) $80\frac{1}{6} - 70\frac{5}{8}$

53) $\left(\frac{9}{70}\right)^3$

54) What is $\frac{1}{8}$ of 4000?

55) What is $\frac{5}{6}$ of 420?

56) What is half of $\frac{7}{9}$?

57) What is half of $\frac{6}{11}$?

58) What is $\frac{3}{7}$ doubled?

59) What is $\frac{3}{16}$ doubled?

60) Reduce $\frac{400}{450}$

61) Reduce $\frac{306}{1980}$

62) Reduce $\frac{1560}{2520}$

Formulas

Temperature conversion formulas:

$$C = \frac{5}{9} \times (F - 32)$$
$$F = \frac{9}{5} \times C + 32$$

63) What is 25°C in Fahrenheit?

64) What is 52°F in Celsius?

Unit cost

65) 6 kg of bananas cost £4.68. How much do 5 kg of bananas cost?

Measurement

66) 5 pounds is how many ounces?

67) 8 feet is how many inches?

68) 1,848,000 cm is how many km?

69) 55 litres of juice is brought on a camping trip. If there are 64 people on the trip, then how much juice is there per person? (Give your answer to the nearest 10 mℓ.)

70) Measure the line below in inches, centimetres and millimetres.

———————————

71) Measure the length of the line that separates the columns on the opposite page, in inches, centimetres, and millimetres.

Sheet 14

Memorised facts

1) 16×3

2) 14^2

3) 16^2

4) Convert $\frac{1}{5}$

5) Convert $\frac{7}{8}$

6) Convert $0.\overline{8}$

7) Convert 0.25

8) 4^4

9) 2^6

10) 5^3

11) 2^4

12) 3^4

Do it in your head

13) 106×109

14) 10.6×1.09

15) 2.15×4

16) $48,000 \div 800$

17) $\left(\frac{7}{11}\right)^2$

18) $\sqrt{12,100}$

19) $21,000 \div 35,000$

20) $40 \div 48$

21) 3×999

22) $9 \times 99,999$

23) Convert $\frac{893}{1000}$

24) Convert $\frac{893}{10,000}$

25) Convert $\frac{893}{999}$

26) Convert $\frac{893}{9990}$

27) Convert $\frac{71}{99,900}$

28) Convert 0.47

29) Convert $0.\overline{47}$

30) Convert $0.0\overline{47}$

31) Convert $0.\overline{047}$

32) Convert $0.000\,\overline{0047}$

Division

33) Leave your answer as a mixed number.
$441,410,000 \div 7000$

Decimals

34) $345.9 + 65.93$

35) $345.9 - 65.93$

36) Cast out nines to check your answer.
345.9×65.93

Fractions

37) Reduce each fraction.
  a) $\frac{28}{30}$

  b) $\frac{7560}{8100}$

  c) $\frac{900}{21,000}$

Formulas

Temperature conversion formulas:

$$C = \frac{5}{9} \times (F - 32)$$
$$F = \frac{9}{5} \times C + 32$$

38) What is $113°F$ in Celsius?

39) What is $52°C$ in Fahrenheit?

40) John works in a bike shop and earns £7.50 per hour plus £9 for every bicycle that he sells. Therefore, the formula that calculates his pay is:
$$P = 7.5 \times H + 9 \times B$$
Where H is the number of hours worked, B is the number of bikes that he sells, and P is his total pay.
  a) How much pay does John earn if he works for 10 hours and sells 3 bikes?

  b) How much pay does he earn if he works for 8 hours and sells 7 bikes?

Making Maths Meaningful

Measurement

41) Give the proper abbreviation for each.

a) yard

b) ounce

c) pound (weight)

d) metre

e) centimetre

f) millimetre

g) kilometre

h) litre

i) millilitre

j) gram

k) milligram

l) kilogram

42) Write a sign ($<$, $>$, $=$) between the two measurements that indicates which one is bigger, or if they are equal.
Example: 1ℓ   2 pt
Since we know that one litre is slightly less than two pints, we write: 1ℓ < 2 pt

a) 1 m   1000 cm
b) 1 mi   2000 yd
c) 36 in   1 yard
d) 1 lb   12 oz
e) 5 g   500 mg
f) 4 ℓ   1 gal
g) 1 g   1000 mg
h) 1 kg   1000 g
i) 1 km   900 m
j) 1 m   120 cm
k) 1 cm   10 mm
l) 5 m   500 cm
m) 7 km   700 m
n) 1 yd   1 m
o) 1 mi   1 km
p) 1 cm   1 in

Converting repeating decimals

Example: Convert $0.147\overline{72}$ into a fraction.
First we realise that
$$0.147\overline{72} = 0.147 + 0.000\,\overline{72}.$$

We know that $0.147 = \frac{147}{1000}$, and that

$0.000\overline{72} = \frac{72}{99,000}$ (don't reduce!)

Since $0.147\overline{72} = 0.147 + 0.000\overline{72}$

we can now say that

$0.147\overline{72} = \frac{147}{1000} + \frac{72}{99,000}$
In order to get a common denominator, we multiply the numerator and denominator of $\frac{147}{1000}$ by 99, giving us $\frac{14,553}{99,000}$.

We now have

$0.147\overline{72} = \frac{14,553}{99,000} + \frac{72}{99,000}$
which adds to $\frac{14,625}{99,000}$.

We reduce this fraction (by dividing the numerator and denominator by 25, 5, and 9) in order to give us a final answer of $\frac{13}{88}$.

Make sure that your work is well organised and readable.

43) a) $0.71\overline{6}$

b) $0.3\overline{18}$

Sheet 15

Memorised facts

1) 13×2

2) 15×3

3) 16×4

4) 18^2

5) Convert $\frac{1}{4}$

6) Convert $\frac{3}{5}$

7) Convert $0.\overline{7}$

8) Convert 0.125

9) 4^3

10) 5^4

11) 2^5

Do it in your head

12) 1100×70

13) 0.0007×100

14) 91×11

15) $600 \div 4$

16) $137 \div 999$

17) $210 \div 240$

18) $800 \div 5$

19) $120 \div 5$

20) $0.7 \div 5$

21) 600^2

22) $\left(\frac{2}{3}\right)^3$

23) $\sqrt{0.09}$

Fractions

24) $\frac{7}{8} + \frac{7}{12}$

25) $\frac{27}{35} + \frac{19}{27}$

26) $\frac{27}{35} \times \frac{19}{27}$

27) $4\frac{3}{8} \div 1\frac{5}{16}$

28) $\dfrac{4\frac{3}{8}}{1\frac{5}{16}}$

29) $\dfrac{1\frac{5}{16}}{4\frac{3}{8}}$

Division

30) Leave your answer as an exact decimal.
$856 \div 2.7$

Formulas

31) On the previous worksheet, review the pay problems about John who works in a bike shop. Use the same formula to do the following problems:

a) How much pay does John earn if he works for 40 hours and sells 11 bikes?

b) John works 22 hours per week. How much pay does he earn if he works for 4 weeks and sells 7 bikes each week?

Measurement

32) State what each abbreviation stands for and about how big it is.

a) m

b) km

c) cm

d) mm

e) ℓ

f) mℓ

g) g

h) kg

i) mg

33) Measure the line below in inches, centimetres and millimetres.
_____

34) As with the previous worksheet, for each of the problems below write a sign (<, >, =) between the two measurements to indicate which one is bigger, or if they are equal.

a) 1 ℓ   1000 mℓ

b) 1 kg   2 lb

c) 7 kg   7000 g

d) 1 m   1000 cm

e) 1 km   5000 m

f) 1 mi   2 km

g) 1 gal   4 ℓ

35) What is the advantage of the metric system?

Unit cost

36) 250 mℓ of maple syrup cost £4.28. How much does one litre of maple syrup cost?

37) Which is a better buy: 1 kg of cheese for £11.95, or the same cheese at a cost of £2.35 for a 200g pack?

Factors

38) List all of the factors:
  a) 100

  b) 144

39) Write down the prime numbers up to 100.

Converting repeating decimals

40) Review the example and the problems given at the end of the previous worksheet, and then convert the following repeating decimals into fractions.
  a) $0.05\overline{2}$

  b) $0.84\overline{459}$

Sheet 16

Do it in your head

1) 25×3 $\begin{array}{r}25\\ \times\ 3\\ \hline 75\end{array}$

2) 18×2 $\begin{array}{r}18\\ \times\ 2\\ \hline 36\end{array}$

3) 14^2 $14 \cdot 14 = 28$ or 392

4) 13×3 $\begin{array}{r}13\\ \times\ 3\\ \hline 39\end{array}$

5) 4^4 $4 \cdot 4 \cdot 4 \cdot 4$ 128

6) 2^3 $2 \cdot 2 \cdot 2$ 8

7) 2^{10} idk

8) $\sqrt{810{,}000}$ 90

9) $(0.011)^2$ 0.022

10) $35 + 2.4$ $\begin{array}{r}35\\ +2.4\\ \hline 5.9\end{array}$

11) $35 - 2.4$ $\begin{array}{r}35\\ -2.4\\ \hline 1.1\end{array}$

12) 0.12×0.03 0.36

13) $0.12 \div 0.03$ 0.04

14) $0.03 \div 0.12$ 0.04

15) $840{,}000 \div 7000$ 1200

16) 7.2×4 28.8

17) 1.07×1.08 115.56

18) $(1.07)^2$ 2.14

19) $3053 - 2987$ 66

I want my summer back!

Making Maths Meaningful

20) 9999×6 59994

21) 64×5 320

22) 4.6×5 23.5

23) $1200 \div 5$ 240

24) $530 \div 5$ 106

25) $1.3 \div 5$ .56

Angle measure

26) First estimate the size of the angle (in degrees), and then use a protractor to measure it. You may need to extend the lines (with a ruler) in order to get a good reading with your protractor.

a)

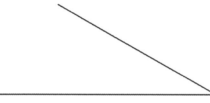

Estimate =
Measurement =

b)
Estimate =
Measurement =

c)

Estimate =
Measurement =

d)

Estimate =
Measurement =

Measurement

27) Estimate the measurement of each object (in metric units).

a) The length of a pencil.

b) The weight of a newborn baby.

c) The volume of a bucket.

d) The distance from one end of town to the other.

e) The thickness of a coin.

f) The weight of a car.

g) The volume of a teacup.

Divisibility

28) State whether each of the following numbers is evenly divisible by 2, 3, 4, 5, 9, or 10.

a) 75,930

b) 1,839,734

Fractions

29) Reduce each fraction:

a) $\dfrac{1040}{1200}$

b) $\dfrac{216,000}{504,000}$

c) $\dfrac{59,625}{91,125}$

30) What is half of $\frac{5}{16}$?

31) What is half of $\frac{6}{17}$?

32) What is $\frac{5}{16}$ doubled?

33) What is $\frac{6}{17}$ doubled?

Conversions

34) Convert to a decimal:
Look through each of the problems below and circle all of the ones you can do in your head. After giving the answers of the ones that you circled, do the others by showing your work on a separate sheet. You'll need to divide for some.

a) $\frac{3}{4}$

b) $\frac{5}{11}$

c) $\frac{61}{100}$

d) $\frac{61}{99}$

e) $\frac{3}{20}$

f) $\frac{2}{11}$

g) $\frac{7}{990}$

h) $\frac{3}{1000}$

i) $\frac{7}{25}$

j) $\frac{131}{400}$

k) $\frac{7}{20}$

l) $\frac{97}{135}$

m) $\frac{3}{8}$

n) $\frac{73}{99,000}$

35) Convert to a fraction:
Circle those that can be done in your head. Note that some of the repeating decimals can be converted to a fraction quite easily in your head, while others follow the method used by the last few problems of the last two worksheets.
As always, answers should be given as reduced fractions.

a) 0.3

b) $0.\overline{5}$

c) 0.5

d) 0.75

e) 0.8

f) 0.0025

g) $0.\overline{1}$

h) $0.8\overline{3}$

i) $0.\overline{65}$

j) $0.\overline{651}$

k) $0.0\overline{07}$

l) $0.00\overline{7}$

m) $0.00\overline{017}$

n) $0.80\overline{5}$

o) $0.03\overline{918}$

p) Challenge!
$0.028\overline{4653}$

Division

36) Leave your answer as a mixed number.

83,745 ÷ 7

37) a) 56

b) 168

c) 14,625

Prime factorisation

Write each number as a product of its prime factors.

Example: 700

$700 = 7 \times 100$

$700 = 7 \times 4 \times 25$

$700 = 7 \times 2 \times 2 \times 5 \times 5$

So our answer is:

$700 = 2^2 \times 5^2 \times 7$

Sheet 17

Do it in your head

1) $25 \times 4 = 100$

2) 16×3 48

3) 15×4 60

4) 13×4 52

5) 2^4 16

6) 3^3 27

7) 4^5 1,024

8) 5000^2 10,000

9) $\sqrt{\frac{4}{25}} = \frac{2}{5}$

10) $\frac{11}{12} - \frac{1}{2} = \frac{5}{12}$

11) $\frac{11}{12} \times \frac{1}{2} = \frac{11}{24}$

12) $\frac{11}{12} \div \frac{1}{2} = \frac{11\cancel{2}^6}{11} \times \frac{1}{\cancel{2}^1} = \frac{6}{11}$

13) $9000 \times 7000 = 63,000,000$

14) $7.34 \div 1000$

15) 560×110

16) $5000 \div 4$ 1,250

17) $56 \div 32$

18) 420×5 2,100

19) $420 \div 5$ 84

Estimate

20) 6839×5182

21) $6839 + 5182$

22) 591^2

Angle measure

23) First estimate the size of the angle (in degrees), and then use a protractor to measure it. You may need to extend the lines (with a ruler) in order to get a good reading with your protractor.

a)

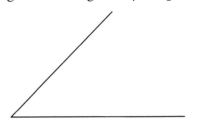

Estimate =
Measurement =

b)

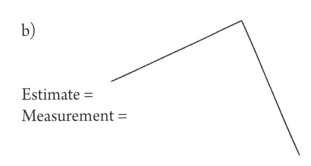

Estimate =
Measurement =

c)

Estimate
Measurement =

d)

Estimate =
Measurement =

Decimals

24) $5080 + 87.42$

25) $5080 - 87.42$

26) Cast out nines to check your answer.
87.54×0.762

Prime factorisation

27) Give the prime factors:

a) 300

b) 2736

c) 816,750

28) Multiply out the prime factors:

a) $2^3 \times 3$

b) $3^2 \times 5 \times 23$

c) $2^4 \times 5^4 \times 13$

Making Maths Meaningful

Conversions

As with the previous worksheet, before doing any of these, circle the ones that can be done in your head.

29) Convert to a decimal:

a) $\frac{5}{8}$

b) $\frac{7}{11}$

c) $\frac{23}{50}$

d) $\frac{23}{30}$

e) $\frac{89}{99}$

f) $\frac{7}{1000}$

g) $\frac{7}{999}$

h) $\frac{7}{900}$

i) $\frac{53}{99,900}$

j) $\frac{29}{270}$

30) Convert to a fraction:

a) $0.\overline{3}$

b) 0.59

c) $0.\overline{59}$

d) 0.059

e) $0.0\overline{59}$

f) $0.0\overline{00059}$

g) $0.\overline{8}$

h) $0.\overline{110}$

i) $0.1\overline{10}$

j) $0.1\overline{6}$

k) $0.31\overline{756}$

31) Convert each fraction into a decimal and a percent:

Example: $\frac{1}{2} = 0.5$ 50%

a) $\frac{1}{4}$

b) $\frac{3}{4}$

c) $\frac{1}{3}$

d) $\frac{2}{3}$

e) $\frac{1}{5}$

f) $\frac{2}{5}$

g) $\frac{3}{5}$

h) $\frac{4}{5}$

i) $\frac{1}{6}$

j) $\frac{5}{6}$

k) $\frac{1}{8}$

l) $\frac{3}{8}$

m) $\frac{5}{8}$

n) $\frac{7}{8}$

o) $\frac{3}{10}$

p) $\frac{7}{10}$

q) $\frac{1}{20}$

r) $\frac{1}{25}$

s) $\frac{1}{50}$

t) $\frac{7}{100}$

u) $\frac{41}{100}$

Percents

32) Convert each percent to a fraction:
 a) 93%

 b) 3%

 c) 15%

 d) 12%

33) Convert each percent to a decimal:
 a) 93%

 b) 3%

 c) 15%

 d) 12.8%

34) What is:
 a) 50% of 280?

 b) 10% of 280?

 c) 25% of 280?

 d) 20% of 280?

 e) 1% of 280?

Sheet 18

Do it in your head

1) 15×5 75

2) 16^2 256

3) 13^2 169

4) 25×6 150

5) Convert $\frac{2}{3}$.$\overline{66}$

6) Convert $\frac{2}{5}$ .4

7) Convert $\frac{56}{99}$.$\overline{56}$

8) Convert $\frac{56}{999}$.$\overline{056}$

9) Convert $\frac{9}{11}$.$\overline{81}$

10) Convert $\frac{1}{20}$ .05

11) Convert $\frac{93}{100} =$ .093

12) Convert $\frac{9}{1000}$ .0009

13) Convert $0.8\overline{3}$

14) Convert 0.875 $\frac{875}{100}$

15) Convert $0.\overline{74}$ $\frac{74}{99}$

16) Convert 0.13

17) Convert 0.0013

18) Convert $0.00\overline{13}$

19) 3^4

20) 2^6

21) 5^3

48

Making Maths Meaningful

22) $24{,}000 \div 600$

23) 5.5×4

24) 0.105×0.108

25) $516 - 497$

26) 5×999

27) 24×99

28) 3.6×5

29) $3.6 \div 5$

30) $\sqrt{64{,}000{,}000}$

31) $\left(\frac{11}{80}\right)^2$

32) $27 + 3.2$

33) $27 - 3.2$

34) 0.4×0.008

35) $0.4 \div 0.008$

Fractions

36) What is half of $\frac{8}{13}$?

37) What is half of $\frac{7}{13}$?

38) What is $\frac{9}{19}$ doubled?

39) What is $\frac{9}{20}$ doubled?

40) $\left(3\frac{1}{8}\right)^2$

41) $46\frac{2}{9} - 28\frac{4}{5}$

42) $\dfrac{5\frac{3}{5}}{1\frac{2}{5}}$

43) $5\frac{3}{5} \div 4$

44) $5\frac{3}{5} \times 4$

Conversions

45) Convert $0.05\overline{30}$ to a fraction.

46) Convert $\frac{59}{444}$ to an exact decimal.

47) For each pair, determine which is bigger and by how much.

 a) $\frac{19}{32}$ and $\frac{5}{8}$

 b) $\frac{1}{7}$ and $\frac{3}{23}$

 c) 58% and 56%

48) What is the advantage of percents?

Statistics

49) Find the *mean, median,* and *mode* of these scores:
    25, 35, 16, 9, 28, 25, 16, 31, 16

Unit cost

50) Eight roses cost £10.32. How much do five roses cost?

Calculating a percentage of a number

Example: What is 60% of 350?

Here are two different methods to solve the problem:

The fraction method
We rephrase the question as: 'What is $\frac{3}{5}$ of 350?' So we do:
$\frac{3}{5} \times 350$, which is 210.

The decimal method
We rephrase the question as: 'What is 0.6 times 350?' So we do:
0.6×350, which is 210.

51) Look at the above example, and then do each question both as a fraction problem and as a decimal problem.
   a) What is 50% of 32?
      Fraction method:

      Decimal method:

   b) What is 25% of 4800?
      Fraction method:

      Decimal method:

   c) What is 75% of 12?
      Fraction method:

      Decimal method:

Percents

52) Convert to a fraction.
   a) 69%

   b) 35%

53) Convert to a decimal.
   a) 53%

   b) 4%

54) Convert to a percent.
   a) 0.81

   b) 0.06

   c) $\frac{47}{100}$

   d) $\frac{4}{5}$

55) 210 is what percent of 350?

Sheet 19

Do it in your head

1) 14×3 42

2) 15^2 225

3) 25×5 125

4) 25^2 625

5) Convert $\frac{1}{8}$ .125

6) Convert $\frac{1}{4}$ .25

7) Convert $\frac{71}{999}$ .071

8) $71 \div 999$

9) Convert $0.\overline{2}$ $\frac{2}{9}$

10) Convert 0.6 $\frac{6}{10}$

11) Convert $0.\overline{07}$ $\frac{7}{90}$

12) 2^5 32

13) 4^3 64

14) 5^4 625

15) 700^2 49,000,000

16) 5.72×1000 4,928

17) 7.6×0.11 .71

18) $0.14 \div 4$ .27

19) $21 \div 33$

Estimate

20) 609×793

21) $6785 \div 89$

22) $23{,}405 - 18{,}482$

Divisibility

23) 1,199,562 is evenly divisible by which: 2, 3, 4, 5, 9, or 10?

Fractions

24) Reduce each fraction.

a) $\frac{112}{256}$

b) $\frac{5175}{17{,}775}$

25) For each pair, determine which is bigger and by how much.

a) $\frac{13}{35}$ and $\frac{3}{8}$

b) 23% and 26%

Angle measure

26) Estimate the size of the angle, and then use a protractor to measure it.

Estimate =
Measurement =

Prime factorisation

27) Give the prime factors:
  a) 720

  b) 99,900

28) Multiply out the prime factors:
  a) $5 \times 11^2 \times 17$

  b) $2^5 \times 3 \times 5^4 \times 11$

Statistics

29) Find the mean, median and mode of these scores:
    210, 230, 460, 250, 280, 170, 110, 180, 140, 250, 190, 220

Calculating a percentage of a number

30) Review the example and the problems from the previous worksheet. Then do each of these problems using either the fraction method or the decimal method, depending upon which is easier.
  a) What is 10% of 3400?

  b) What is 50% of 48?

c) What is 21% of 450?

d) What is 20% of 750?

e) What is 75% of 1200?

f) What is 33⅓% of 6000?

g) What is 39% of 700?

h) What is 25% of 44?

Percents

31) Convert to a fraction:
  a) 73%

  b) 46%

32) Convert to a decimal:
  a) 28%

  b) 9%

33) Convert to a percent:
  a) 0.7

  b) 0.07

  c) $\frac{23}{100}$

  d) $\frac{3}{4}$

Determining the percentage

Example: 15 is what percent of 25?
This question can be answered in three ways:

Method 1

If the fraction is (or reduces to) something that we have memorised the percentage for:

$\frac{15}{25}$ reduces to $\frac{3}{5}$, which is 60%.

Method 2

If the denominator can easily be changed to 100:

With $\frac{15}{25}$ we multiply top and bottom by 4 to get $\frac{60}{100}$, which is 60%.

Method 3

Otherwise, convert to a decimal by dividing.

With $\frac{15}{25}$ we divide 25 into 15, which is 0.6 or 60%.

Note: Method 3 is always possible, but should be used only if the first two methods aren't possible.

34) Study the above example and then do each of these:
   a) 43 is what percent of 50?

   b) 320 is what percent of 400?

   c) 388 is what percent of 400?

   d) 450 is what percent of 720?

   e) 90 is what percent of 750?

Pie charts

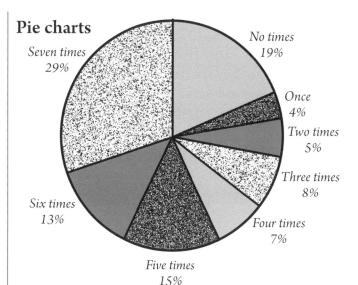

35) The above pie chart shows the result of a survey of 800 people who were asked how many times per week they typically eat breakfast at home.
   Answer the following.
   a) What is the number of people (out of the 800 surveyed) that eat breakfast at home every day?

   b) What percentage of the people eat breakfast at home at least 5 days per week?

   c) What is the number of people that eat breakfast at home at least 5 days per week?

   d) Is the following statement true or false? More people eat breakfast at home every day than eat breakfast at home either two, three, or four times per week.

Sheet 20

Do it in your head

1) $160,000 \div 2000$

2) 8.55×4

3) 1110×1080

4) $6043 - 4996$

5) 9999×7

6) 999×18

7) 6400×5

8) $6400 \div 5$

9) 15×2

10) 16×4

11) 15×3

12) 18^2

13) 4^4

14) 2^3

15) 2^{10}

Convert to a percent

16) $\frac{1}{2}$

17) $\frac{4}{5}$

18) $\frac{3}{8}$

19) 0.3

20) 0.736

Convert to a fraction

21) 75%

22) 23%

23) 16%

24) 2%

Fractions

25) Convert to a fraction:

a) 0.893

b) 0.875

c) $0.8\overline{3}$

d) 0.00025

e) 0.0268

f) $0.\overline{162}$

26) $3\frac{5}{6} \times 100$

27) $\dfrac{6\frac{2}{3}}{4}$

28) $\dfrac{7}{80} + \dfrac{11}{120}$

Making Maths Meaningful

29) $68\frac{2}{15} - \frac{5}{6}$

30) $\left(4\frac{1}{2}\right)^3$

31) What is $\frac{2}{5}$ of $6\frac{1}{4}$?

Decimals
32) $38.7 - 0.0914$

33) $(0.0052)^2$

34) Convert to a fraction:
$0.049\overline{24}$

Measurement
35) 6 litres is how many millilitres?

36) 6 pints is how many gallons?

37) 120 mℓ is how many litres?

38) 279 cm is how many metres?

39) 10½ tons of compost is to be divided evenly between 60 gardens. How many kg of compost does each garden get?

Calculating a percentage of a number
40) Use the easiest method.
   a) What is 10% of 940?

   b) What is 1% of 940?

   c) What is 9% of 250?

   d) What is 80% of 45?

   e) What is 25% of 12,000?

Determining the percentage
41) Review the example from the previous worksheet, and then answer these questions:
   a) 60 is what percent of 150?

   b) 180 is what percent of 480?

   c) 21 is what percent of 25?

   d) 47 is what percent of 120?

Increase/decrease
42) a) What is 300 increased by 50%?

   b) What is 60 increased by 20%?

   c) What is 2000 increased by 15%?

Area and perimeter

43) Calculate the area and perimeter of each rectangle.

a)

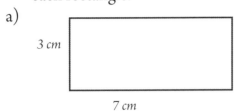

3 cm

7 cm

Perimeter =

Area =

b)

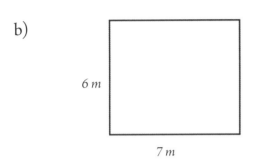

6 m

7 m

Perimeter =

Area =

Pie charts

44) At Happy School 250 people were surveyed about how they usually get to school. The results were:

120 by bus

55 by car

45 by walking

30 by other means

Review the pie chart from the previous worksheet. Construct a similar pie chart, in the space below, that uses the data from the above survey, where each of the pie pieces are shaded in using a different color. The angles of the pie pieces should be calculated exactly and constructed using a protractor.

Sheet 21

Do it in your head

1) 120×90

2) $7649 \div 100$

3) 0.87×11

4) 25×3

5) $6.4 \div 4$

6) $220 \div 330$

7) 14^2

8) 13×3

9) 25×2

10) 2^4

11) 3^3

12) 4^5

13) $\sqrt{0.0049}$

14) 9000^2

15) Convert to a percent:
 a) $\frac{1}{5}$

 b) 0.61

 c) $\frac{5}{8}$

16) Convert to a fraction:
 a) $0.\overline{3}$

 b) 40%

 c) $16\frac{2}{3}\%$

17) Convert to a decimal:

 a) $\frac{4}{99}$

 b) 87%

 c) 6%

Area and perimeter

18) Calculate the area and perimeter.
 a)

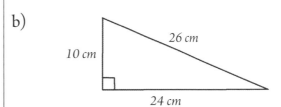

$3\frac{1}{2}\,m$

$5\,m$

Perimeter =

Area =

 b)

$26\,cm$

$10\,cm$

$24\,cm$

Perimeter =

Area =

Statistics

19) Find the mean, median and mode of these scores:
7, 3, 23, 9, 5, 16, 5, 3, 16, 3, 9, 7, 9, 18, 8, 11, 4.

Fractions, decimals & percents

20) What is $\frac{3}{8}$ of $4\frac{5}{6}$?

21) $(0.2)^{10}$

22) Convert to a fraction:
   a) 0.72

   b) 0.015

   c) 0.468

   d) 74%

   e) 81.25%

23) Convert to a percent:
   a) 0.96

   b) 0.05

   c) 0.1

   d) 0.873

   e) $\frac{7}{50}$

   f) $\frac{43}{60}$

24) What is 60% of 65?

25) What is 73% of 680?

26) What is $33\frac{1}{3}$% of 12,000?

27) What is $12\frac{1}{2}$% of 240?

28) What is $16\frac{2}{3}$% of 72?

29) 7 is what percent of 35?

30) 18 is what percent of 75?

31) 450 is what percent of 540?

32) 43 is what percent of 60?

33) The previous problem is the same as which other problem on this worksheet?

34) What is 2400 decreased by 21%?

35) What is 40 increased by $62\frac{1}{2}$%?

Business maths

36) A bicycle in a shop is marked at £260. What do you pay if the delivery charge is 7%?

37) Bill can make a chair at a cost of £36, including parts and labour. What must his selling price be (rounded to the nearest pound) if he wants to make a 30% profit?

38) A clothing shop is having a 35%-off sale. What is the new discounted price of a jacket that was originally marked at £120?

Sheet 22

Do it in your head

1) 13×4

2) 25×4

3) 16×3

4) 15×4

5) 3^4

6) 2^6

7) 5^3

8) $18,000 \div 2000$

9) 10.9^2

10) $235,000 \times 4$

11) $3243 - 2987$

12) 8×999.99

13) 15×999

14) 6200×5

15) $740 \div 5$

16) $21 - 3.1$

17) $0.03 \div 0.0006$

18) $\sqrt{6400}$

19) Convert to a percent:
a) $\frac{2}{5}$

b) $\frac{1}{6}$

c) 0.94

d) 0.9

e) $\frac{2}{3}$

20) Convert to a fraction:
a) $0.\overline{38}$

b) $87\frac{1}{2}\%$

c) 80%

21) Convert to a decimal:
  a) $\frac{8}{999}$

  b) 52%

  c) 5%

Prime factorisation
Give the prime factors:
22) 875

23) 309,600

24) Multiply out the prime factors:
$2^4 \times 3^2 \times 5^4 \times 11$

Fractions, decimals & percents
25) Convert to *both* a mixed number and an exact decimal.
  a) $\frac{58}{11}$

  b) $\frac{48,683}{8}$

26) Convert to a fraction:
  a) 0.55

  b) 0.344

  c) 69%

  d) 42¾%

27) Convert to a percent:
  a) 0.26

  b) 0.073

  c) $\frac{13}{20}$

28) What is 25% of 32?

29) What is 62% of 850?

30) What is 5% of 12,000?

31) What is 87½% of 48?

32) 130 is what percent of 260?

33) 180 is what percent of 270?

34) 59 is what percent of 150?

35) What is 35 decreased by 60%?

36) What is 58 decreased by 7%?

Business maths

37) A shop is having a 60%-off sale. What is the new discounted price of a shirt that was originally marked at £35?

38) The previous problem is the same as which other problem on this worksheet?

39) An estate agent makes a 2% commission when he sells a house. How much does he earn if he sells a house for £348,000?

40) 750 grams of cheese cost £4.68. How much does 3 kg of that same cheese cost?

41) John earns £8.50/hr. How much does he earn in a 40-hour week?

42) Cathy earned £400 and worked 32 hours last week. What was her hourly wage?

Sheet 23

Do it in your head

1) 13^2

2) 15×5

3) 16^2

4) 25×6

5) 2^5

6) 4^3

7) 5^4

8) 400^2

9) 0.00026×100

10) 0.11×0.53

11) $0.22 \div 4$

12) $59 \div 99$

13) $32 \div 48$

14) $\sqrt{\dfrac{121}{3600}}$

15) $\frac{2}{3} - \frac{1}{4}$

16) $\frac{4}{15} \times \frac{5}{12}$

17) $\frac{7}{13} \div \frac{7}{13}$

18) Convert to a percent:
 a) ¼

 b) ⅛

 c) 0.46

 d) 0.8

19) Convert to a fraction:
 a) 60%

 b) 23%

 c) 23.7%

 d) $55\frac{5}{9}\%$

 e) 0.05

20) Convert to a decimal:
 a) 84%

 b) 4.6%

 c) $\frac{2}{11}$

 d) $\frac{3}{20}$

Area and perimeter
21) Calculate the area and perimeter of each.
 a)

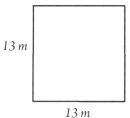

13 m

13 m

Perimeter =

Area =

b)

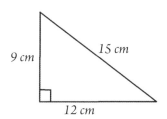

9 cm   15 cm

12 cm

Perimeter =

Area =

Divisibility
22) Which numbers is 2,541,280 evenly divisible by: 2, 3, 4, 5, 9, or 10?

Fractions
23) Reduce each fraction:

 a) $\frac{9600}{43,200}$

 b) $\frac{912}{9828}$

Measurement
24) 3½ kg = _____ g

25) 81 mm = _____ m

26) 4 ℓ = _____ mℓ

27) 3 km = _____ cm

28) 31¼ tonnes = _____ kg

Percents
29) Convert 15.6% to a fraction.

30) What is 40% of 320?

31) What is 7% of 61?

32) 140 is what percent of 160?

33) 140 is what percent of 150?

34) What is 240 increased by 33⅓%?

Ratios
35) There are 12 girls and 15 boys in Kate's class.
   a) What is the ratio of boys to girls?

   b) What is the ratio of girls to boys?

36) John has 28 cows and 126 sheep on his farm. What is the ratio of cows to sheep?

Pay rate, speed, etc.
37) Fred's hourly wage is £11.25 per hour.
   a) What does Fred earn in a 40-hour work-week?

   b) What does Fred earn in a year? (Assume that he works 50 weeks in a year.)

38) Kate is paid £60/day. How long does it take her to earn £720?

39) Bill earns £356 in a 40-hour week. What is his hourly wage?

40) Karen cycles at a rate of 12 km/h.
   a) How far does she go in 5 hours?

   b) How far does she go in 3½ hours?

   c) How long does it take her to go 36 km?

Sheet 24

Do it in your head

1) 14×3

2) 15^2

3) 25×5

4) 2^3

5) 4^4

6) 2^{10}

7) $72{,}000 \div 60$

8) 1030×1050

9) $736 - 677$

10) 35×999

11) 216×5

12) $216 \div 5$

13) $\sqrt{3600}$

14) $\left(\frac{3}{25}\right)^2$

15) Convert to a percent:
 a) $\frac{3}{4}$

 b) $\frac{3}{8}$

 c) 0.7

16) Convert to a fraction:
 a) 80%

 b) 17%

 c) 0.002

 d) $0.\overline{52}$

17) Convert to a decimal:
 a) $\frac{6}{11}$

 b) 62%

Fractions, decimals & percents

18) $0.045 - 0.00032$

19) 0.045×0.00032

20) $0.045 \div 0.00032$

21) $0.00005 \div 0.004$

22) $\frac{67}{90} - \frac{14}{40}$

23) $\frac{24}{36} \times \frac{25}{35}$

24) $5 \div 3\frac{4}{5}$

25) What is 83% of 250?

26) What is 37½% of 8?

27) 14 is what percent of 42?

28) 13 is what percent of 90?

29) ¾ is what percent of 4½?

30) Jim's meal at the Yummy Plate restaurant cost £23.00. What was his total cost if he left a 12% tip?

31) Mary bought a house for £160,000 and sold it 10 years later at a 75% profit. How much did she sell the house for?

32) John bought a new car for £31,500 and then sold it a year later at a 30% loss. How much did he sell the car for and how much money did he lose?

Ratios

33) There are 275 students and 25 teachers at Southern Midland School. What is the student-to-teacher ratio?

34) A recipe calls for 2 litres of water, 3 eggs, 1250 mℓ of flour, and 2 teaspoons of salt. What is the ratio of flour to water?

Pay rate, speed, etc.

35) A plane is travelling at 980 km/h.
   a) How far does the plane go in 3 hours?

   b) How far does the plane go in 5½ hours?

   c) How long does it take the plane to go 4800 km? (Round your answer to the nearest minute.)

36) What is Betty's average speed if …
   a) she cycles 48 km in 3 hours?

   b) she bikes 48 km in 3 hours 15 minutes? (Round your answer to three significant digits.)

Line graphs

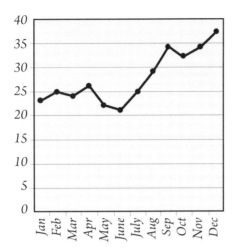

The above graph shows the amount of sales (in thousands of pounds) at Kate's Bike Shop during last year.

37) Which month had the least amount of sales, and what was the amount of sales in that month?

38) Which month had the greatest amount of sales, and what was the amount of sales in that month?

39) Which period of time had the greatest growth in sales?

40) Which period of time had the greatest drop in sales?

41) For which period of time was sales relatively constant?

Sheet 25

Do it in your head

1) 15×3

2) 16×4

3) 18^2

4) 3^3

5) 2^4

6) 4^5

7) 1.1×6.9

8) $6 \div 1000$

9) $150 \div 240$

10) 1800^2

11) $\sqrt{0.04}$

12) Convert to a percent:
 a) $\frac{5}{8}$

 b) $\frac{5}{6}$

 c) $0.\overline{8}$

13) Convert to a fraction:
 a) 20%

 b) $33\frac{1}{3}\%$

 c) 0.004

14) Convert to a decimal:
 a) $\frac{9}{20}$

 b) $38.\overline{4}\%$

c) $9\frac{1}{2}\%$

d) $4\frac{1}{3}\%$

Foreign exchange

Quick Bank has its foreign exchange rates posted as:

US Dollar ($)
    Buy $1.45 / £
    Sell $1.35 / £
Euros (€)
    Buy €1.25 / £
    Sell €1.15 / £

Tips for doing foreign exchange rate problems:

- Whenever an exchange of foreign currency takes place between a bank and a customer, each party is buying one currency and selling the other currency.
- If you are buying euros from the bank, you are also selling pounds to the bank. At that same moment, the bank is selling euros and buying pounds.
- The exchange rates listed at any bank are always given in terms of whether the bank is selling or buying the foreign currency, not whether you are buying or selling the foreign currency.
- *To do a foreign exchange calculation, you must answer three questions:*
1. Which currency is worth more?
2. Is the bank buying or selling the foreign currency?
3. Should we divide or multiply by the given rate?

Example: At Quick Bank, how many euros do you get for £50?

    Answering the three questions, we get:
1. A pound is worth more than a euro.
2. The bank is selling euros.
3. Since the selling rate for euros is 1.15, we can see that we must multiply 50 by 1.15, resulting in an answer of 57.50 euros.

    If we had mistakenly divided 50 by 1.15,

we would have had an answer of €43.48, which would obviously not be a good deal.

15) At Quick Bank, how many pounds do you get for 200 euros?

16) How many US dollars do you get for £380?

17) How many euros do you need to give the bank in order to get £80?

Fractions, decimals & percents

18) $13 - 4\frac{3}{11}$

19) $\dfrac{6}{6\frac{2}{5}}$

20) What is 9% of 230?

21) What is $16\frac{2}{3}\%$ of 42?

22) 62 is what percent of 487? (Round your answer to three significant digits.)

Ratios

23) What is the ratio of men to women in a university that has approximately 2700 men and 2250 women?

Pay rate, speed, etc.

24) Jane earned £363.20 in 32 hours of work. What is her hourly wage?

25) A train is travelling at 75 km/h.
 a) How far does the train go in 4 hours and 20 minutes?

 b) How long does it take the train to go 200 km?

Line graphs

26) The graph below shows the rate at which Mike did his maths homework. Describe specifically what the graph shows.

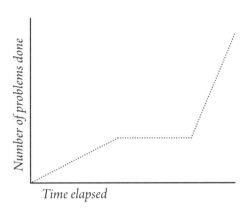

27) Review the line graph from the end of the previous worksheet. Construct, as neatly and accurately as possible, a similar line graph given the data below of the population of Boulder, Colorado. You will need to carefully measure the intervals along the vertical and horizontal axes. (Note the time intervals change!)

Boulder's population

Year	Population
1920	11,006
1930	11,223
1940	12,958
1950	19,999
1960	37,718
1965	51,000
1970	66,870
1975	79,000
1980	76,685
1985	83,000
1990	83,312
1995	96,000
2000	94,673

Sheet 26

Do it in your head

1) 2.5×3

2) 0.16×2

3) 1.4^2

4) 1.3×3

5) 3^4

6) 5^3

7) $(0.2)^6$

8) 0.106×0.105

9) $80,000 \div 50$

10) $724 - 487$

11) 3×99

12) 16×99

13) 234×5

14) $0.234 \div 0.05$

15) $\sqrt{40,000}$

16) Convert to a percent:
   a) $\frac{2}{3}$

   b) $\frac{7}{8}$

   c) $\frac{2}{5}$

   d) $\frac{1}{6}$

17) Convert to a fraction:
   a) 90%

   b) 15%

   c) 37.5%

18) Convert to a decimal:
   a) $\frac{5}{11}$

   b) 3.7%

Percents

19) What is 42% of 600?

20) What is 12½% of 320?

21) 15 is what percent of 60?

22) 31 is what percent of 37? (Round your answer to three significant digits.)

23) How much do you have to pay for having a £48 jacket altered if there is 9% surcharge for this?

Ratios

24) At a train station in Holland there are 975 bikes parked and 75 cars. What is the ratio of bikes to cars?

Pay rate, speed, etc.

25) Fran's hourly wage is £12/hr and she works 32 hours per week. How long does it take her to earn £2400?

Compound fractions

26) $\dfrac{3 - \frac{1}{4}}{\frac{5}{6} \times 2\frac{1}{2}}$

27) $\dfrac{2}{2 - \dfrac{2}{2 - \frac{1}{2}}}$

Foreign exchange

Review the foreign exchange example and problems from the previous worksheet.

The rates for the US dollar at Quick Bank in England are:

Buy $1.45/£

Sell $1.35/£

The exchange rates for the pound at Express Bank (in USA) are:

Buy £0.75/$

Sell £0.67/$

28) Which bank do you think has better rates for its customers?

29) How many dollars do you get for £200 at Express Bank?

30) How many pounds do you need to give Quick Bank in order to get $400?

31) At each bank, what do you end up with if you change £150 into dollars, and then change that back into pounds? (Note: banks don't usually give coins in foreign currency.)

a) At Quick Bank:

b) At Express Bank:

32) Now, which bank do you think has better rates?

Line graphs
33) The graphs show the rates at which two people mowed two same sized lawns.

   Given that both Kate and John mowed their lawn in the same amount of time, describe the differences that are shown in the graphs.

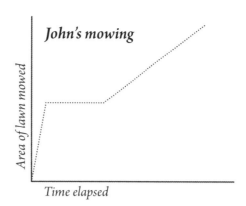

John's mowing

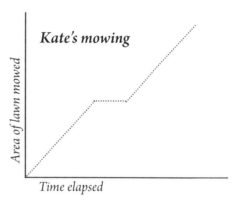

Kate's mowing

Sheet 27

Do it in your head

1) 25×4

2) 1.5×4

3) 0.16×3

4) 130×4

5) 5^4

6) 20^5

7) $(0.4)^3$

8) 7000^2

9) 7.362×100

10) 1.1×8.8

11) $900 \div 4$

12) $8 \div 999$

13) $4800 \div 5400$

14) $\sqrt{\dfrac{49}{810,000}}$

15) $\dfrac{3}{11} \times \dfrac{4}{11}$

16) $\dfrac{3}{11} \div \dfrac{4}{11}$

17) $\dfrac{3}{11} + \dfrac{4}{11}$

18) $\dfrac{3}{11} + \dfrac{3}{8}$

19) Convert to a percent:

a) ⅗

b) ¼

c) $\frac{5}{9}$

d) $\frac{1}{8}$

20) Convert 6% to a fraction.

Percents

21) What is 83⅓% of 120?

22) What is 2% of 510?

23) 3500 is what percent of 5600?

24) A pair of skis at a sports shop is normally priced at £475. What is the new discounted price if the shop is having a 40%-off sale?

Unit cost

25) A hotel room costs £130 for four days. What does it cost for a full week?

Pay rate, speed, etc.

26) The Skip bus is scheduled to leave Lee Hill at 3:27 and to arrive at the University, 5½ km away, at 3:47. What is the bus's average speed?

27) The Thalys train is scheduled to depart from Brussels Midi at 7:11 and then to arrive at Paris Nord at 8:35. What is the average speed for the trip given that the distance between the two stations is 336 km?

Compound fractions

28) $\dfrac{\frac{5}{8}-\frac{1}{3}}{7-\dfrac{8}{2\frac{1}{7}\times 2\frac{4}{5}}}$

29) $\dfrac{2\frac{1}{3}-\dfrac{\frac{1}{2}+\frac{1}{3}}{2}-\frac{1}{4}\times\frac{1}{3}}{\dfrac{1}{2-\frac{4}{5}}+1}$

30) $\dfrac{3}{3-\dfrac{3}{3-\frac{3}{3-\frac{1}{3}}}}$

Foreign exchange

Quick Bank's foreign exchange rates are:

US Dollar ($)

    Buy $1.45 / £   *Sell $1.35 / £*

Euros (€)

    Buy €1.25 / £   *Sell €1.15 / £*

    At Express Bank (in USA) they are:

    Buy £0.75/$*   *Sell £0.67/$

31) At Quick Bank, how many pounds do you get for €200?

32) At Quick Bank, how many euros do you need to pay in order to get £300?

33) At Express Bank, how many pounds do you get for $380?

34) At Express Bank, how many pounds do you need to pay in order to get $380?

35) Speedy Bank (across the road from Quick Bank) has its rates posted as:
    Buy $1.46/£
    Sell $1.34/£
Should you exchange dollars into pounds at Speedy or at Quick Bank?

Line graphs

Review the line graphs from the previous sheet.

36) Explain why the graph below would be impossible.

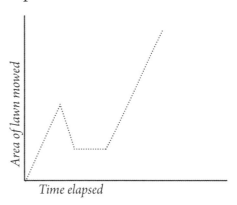

37) Explain how the graph below could show the progress during Jane's cycling trip.

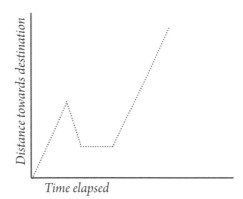

Looking for the answers?

A PDF of the teacher's answer booklet is available on request from Floris Books. Please email floris@florisbooks.co.uk stating which class answer booklet you require.

Class Six Maths Tricks

Multiplication and zeros. When multiplying two numbers, ignore all ending zeros, do the multiplication, and then add the zeros back onto the answer.

Example: For 4000×300,
we multiply 4 times 3,
and then add on the 5 zeros
giving a result of 1,200,000.

Division and zeros. When dividing two numbers that both end in zeros, cancel the same number of ending zeros from each of the two numbers, then do the division problem.

Example: For $24,000 \div 600$,
we cancel two zeros from both numbers,
and then divide 240 by 6 to get 40.

Multiplying and dividing by 10, 100, 1000, etc. Simply move the decimal point!

Example: $634.6 \div 100 = 6.346$
We move the decimal point 2 places
because there are 2 zeros in 100.

Example: $48.37 \times 1000 = 48370$
The decimal point gets moved 3 places
since there are 3 zeros in 1000.

Adding numbers by grouping. Search for digits that add up to 10 or 20.

Example: For $97 + 86 + 13 + 42 + 54$,
we see that with the units' digits we can add
$7 + 3$ and $6 + 4$ to make ten twice,
leaving the 2 (from the 42) left over.
The sum of the units' column is therefore 22.
In the tens' column, the carry of 2 combines with the 8 to form 10, as does the 9 and the 1.
We are left with the 4 and 5.
The tens' column is therefore 29.
Our answer is 292.

Multiplying by 4. You can instead double the number two times.

Example: For 4×35,
we double 35 to get 70,
and double again to get a result of 140.

Multiplying a 2-digit number by 11. Separate the digits, and then insert the sum of the digits in-between.

Example: For 62×11,
6 plus 2 is 8,
so we place the 8 between the 6 and the 2,
giving a result of 682.

Example: For 75×11,
7 plus 5 is 12,
so we place the 2 between the 7 and 5
and carry the 1, giving 825.

Multiplying two numbers that are just over 100. First write down a 1, then next to the one we write down the sum of how far above 100 the two numbers are, and then the product of how far above 100 the two numbers are. Both the sum and the product must be two digits.

Example: For 105×102,
add 5 plus 2 (to get 07),
and then multiply 5 times 2 (to get 10),
giving 10,710.

Example: For 112×107,
we do $12 + 7$ (19)
and then 12×7 (84),
which leads to an answer of 11,984.

Dividing by 4. You can instead cut the number in half, two times.

Example: For $64 \div 4$,
we take half of 64 to get 32,
and then take half of that
for a result of 16.

Subtraction by adding distances. Pick an 'easy' number between the two numbers, and add the distances from each of the numbers to the easy number.

Example: For 532 − 497,
choose 500 as the easy number.
The distance from 532 to 500 is 32
and the distance from 497 to 500 is 3.
The answer is therefore 32+3, which is 35.

Division by nines. When dividing two numbers where the divisor's digits are all nines, we get a decimal where the dividend repeats, but the number of repeating digits must be equal to the number of nines.

Example: $38 \div 99 = 0.\overline{38}$
Example: $417 \div 999 = 0.\overline{417}$
Example: $62 \div 999 = 0.\overline{062}$

Multiplying by nines.
Method 1: Multiply by 10, 100, or 1000, and then subtract the original number.

Example: For 47 × 99,
we do 100 × 47 − 47,
which is 4700−47,
giving an answer of 4653.

Method 2 (for single digits): Multiply the single digit by 9, which gives us a two-digit answer. Then separate these two digits and insert one less nine than what was in the original problem.

Example: For 8 × 9999,
we multiply 8 times 9,
which gives us 72.
Then we insert three nines
between the 7 and the 2,
giving a final answer of 79,992.

Reducing before dividing. Any division problem is viewed as a fraction that can often be reduced.

Example: For 3500÷2800,
we reduce the fraction to 5/4,
which is 1¼ or 1.25.

Multiplying by 5. Take half the number, and then add a zero, or move the decimal point.

Example: For 5 × 26,
we take half of 26 to get 13,
and then add a zero,
giving us a result of 130.

Example: For 5 × 4.18,
half of 4.18 is 2.09,
and moving the decimal point
to the right one place gives 20.9.

Dividing by 5. Double the number, and then divide by ten (move the decimal one place to the left).

Example: For 80 ÷ 5,
we double 80
and then chop off a zero,
giving a result of 16.

Example: For 93 ÷ 5,
we double 93
and then move the decimal point
one place to the left to get 18.6.

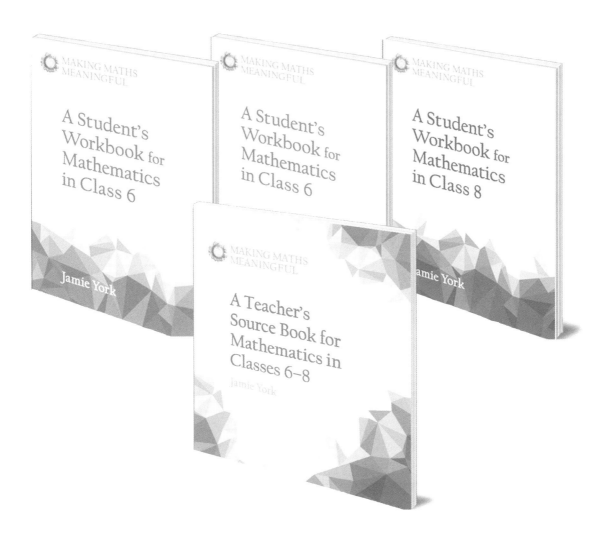

Jamie York's unique maths workbooks are available for Classes 6, 7 and 8, alongside a comprehensive teacher's book for all three years.

"Jamie York has helped me develop students who are on the path to becoming imaginative, analytical thinkers in high school."
– Waldorf teacher, Portland, Oregon

florisbooks.co.uk

Fun with Maths Puzzles, Games and More

A Resource Book for Steiner-Waldorf Teachers

Jamie York, Randy Evans and Mick Follari

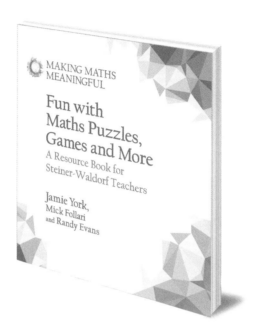

An inspirational and easy-to-use resource book for teachers who want to add interest and engagement to maths lessons. Part of the acclaimed Making Maths Meaningful series.

The puzzles, games and activities in this book are designed to challenge students with new ways of applying core maths skills. Created by experienced maths teachers, with a focus on problem solving rather than solving problems, teachers will find activities to supplement all main maths topics – from addition and subtraction to algebra and logic puzzles.

Discover the perfect puzzle to inspire your class with this clear and easy-to-use resource.

florisbooks.co.uk

String, Straight-edge and Shadow
The Story of Geometry

Julia E. Diggins

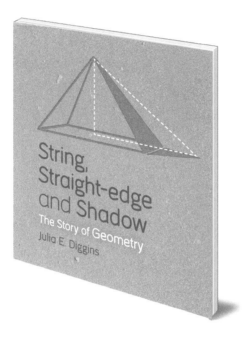

From the early peoples who marvelled at the geometry of nature – the beehive and bird's nest – to ancient civilisations who questioned beautiful geometric forms and asked 'why?', the story of geometry spans thousands of years.

Using only three simple tools – the string, the straight-edge and the shadow – human beings revealed the basic principles and constructions of elementary geometry. Weaving history and legend, this fascinating book reconstructs the discoveries of mathematics's most famous figures. Through illustrations and diagrams, readers are able to follow the reasoning that lead to an ingenious proof of the Pythagorean theorem, an appreciation of the significance of the Golden Mean in art and architecture, or the construction of the five regular solids.

This insightful and engaging book is a useful and inspiring book for those teaching geometry in Steiner-Waldorf classrooms.

florisbooks.co.uk

Floris Books

For news on all our **latest books,**
and to receive **exclusive discounts,**
join our mailing list at:

florisbooks.co.uk/signup

Plus subscribers get a FREE book
with every online order!

We will never pass your details to anyone else.